George Washington's

RULES OF CIVILITY
& DECENT BEHAVIOR

...AND OTHER WRITINGS

SOURCEBOOKS, INC.®
NAPERVILLE, ILLINOIS

Published by Sourcebooks, Inc.

P.O. Box 4410, Naperville, Illinois 60567-4410

(630) 961-3900

Fax: (630) 961-2168

www.sourcebooks.com

Printed and bound in the United States of America.

WZ 10 9 8 7 6 5 4 3 2

A Life of Virtue and a Leader of Legend 1

The Rules of Civility 7

Farewell to the Armies 121

Army Retirement Address 133

Washington's First Inaugural Address 137

Address at the End of His Presidency 147

,

...your union ought to be considered as a main prop of your liberty, and that the love of the one ought to endear to you the preservation of the other.

— ADDRESS AT THE END OF HIS PRESIDENCY,

NEW YORK CITY, SEPTEMBER 19, 1796

A Life of Virtue
AND A LEADER OF LEGEND

❧

I^{T IS PERHAPS THE DEFINING} moment of the United States, the most shining and influential example of the nobility and character of the American people. After the Revolutionary War, when he could have accepted the throne that the officers who had served beneath him during his victory over the British were so eager to have him assume, George Washington humbly refused the monarchy, quelled the movement of his officers to give him the crown, and returned to his plantation to live as a tobacco farmer.

Of course, Washington was not permitted the sedate life of farmer and family man—a life he so desperately craved—for long. In 1787 he was called out of retirement to preside at the Constitutional Convention; two years later, he was the first president of the United States of America (the first and only president to be elected unanimously by the Electoral College, a feat he duplicated in 1792).

Throughout his life and certainly during his time as the country's most influential leader, Washington was known as a remarkably modest and courteous man. Humility and flawless manners were so ingrained in his character that he rarely if ever acted without them (despite his famously short temper); and historians have long speculated that one particular school exercise, completed before he was sixteen years old, had such an impact that it shaped and affected his character and actions for the duration of his life.

That school exercise was, of course, copying 110 maxims for proper behavior, *Rules of Civility and Decent Behavior*, the very same text you're holding in your hands right now. The rules themselves are ancient; they have been traced back to a longer work on etiquette, *Bienseance de la Conversation entre les Hommes* (*Decency of Conversation among Men*) written by Jesuit scholars in the late sixteenth century. The book was written at the College of La Fleche in the western French city of La Fleche (which still exists as a school today, the Prytanée National Militaire).

The book was sent on to a monastery in northeastern France, Pont-a-Mousson, where it was translated into Latin in 1617. The translator, a Father Perin, added his own chapter on table manners. The Latin edition appeared in Paris in 1638.

In 1640, *Youths Behavior, or Decency in Conversation amoungst Men,* was published in English in London. The translator was listed as eight-year-old Francis Hawkins (whether or not the rules were actually translated by so young a boy is debatable). As a testament to the rules' influence and popularity, the book went through at least eleven editions over the next few decades and was even published as *Youth's Behaviour, or Decency in Conversation amongst Women* by a Puritan bookmaker, Robert Codrington, in 1664.

It is not precisely known how the rules got to Colonial Virginia and into the hands and mind of the young George Washington, though it is possible that his father or one of his half-brothers—all of whom were educated in England—brought a copy back to Virginia. What is known is that the code of honor, respect, and courteous behavior that the maxims espouse was embodied to perfection in the first president of the United States. Imagine the difficulties faced by George Washington, the military man who wanted nothing more than to retire to a sedate and quiet life on his familial plantation. Not only did it fall to him to refuse the absolute power of the monarchy or military dictatorship within his grasp—a monumental and almost unimaginable rejection—but he also had to set the example for a new and powerful office and create a precedent for the behavior of a kind of leader the world had never seen. And instead of ruling by fear or exploiting the as-of-yet unestablished laws limiting the power of his office, Washington employed the system of courtesy and respect that rules penned by Jesuits in another country, in another age, had ingrained in him.

Now, you can discover these tips for proper social conduct that formed the man who, in turn, formed a great nation. George Washington is a man admired not just because of his political policies, but also his personal convictions. In the words of Parson Weems, the contemporary of Washington's who is one of his most famous biographers (and the author of the unproven, charming allegory of the cherry tree):

O admirable man! O great preceptor to his country! No wonder everybody honored him who honored everybody; for the poorest beggar that wrote to him on business, was sure to receive a speedy and decisive answer. No wonder everybody loved him who, by his unwearied attention to the public good, manifested the tenderest love for everybody.

—A HISTORY OF THE LIFE AND DEATH, VIRTUES
AND EXPLOITS OF GENERAL GEORGE WASHINGTON
BY PARSON WEEMS (1800)

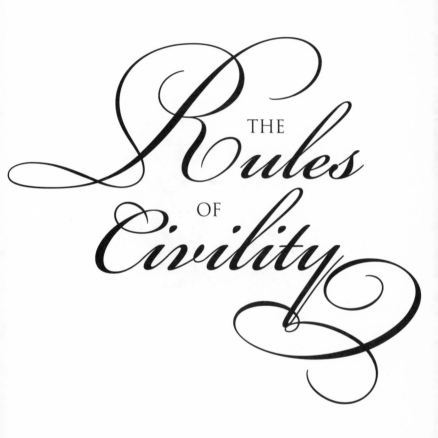

THE

OF

Rules

Civility

1

Every action
done in company
ought to be done
with some sign
of respect
to those that
are present.

2

When in company,
put not your hands
to any part
of the body
not usually discovered.

3

Show nothing
to your friend that
may affright him.

4

In the presence of others
sing not to yourself
with a humming noise,
nor drum with your
fingers or feet.

5

If you cough,
sneeze, sigh, or yawn,
do it not loud but privately;
and speak not in your yawning,
but put your handkerchief
or hand before your face
and turn aside.

6

Sleep not
when others speak,
sit not when others stand,
speak not when you
should hold your peace,
walk not on when
others stop.

7

Put not off your clothes
in the presence of others,
nor go out
of your chamber
half-dressed.

8

At play and at fire
it is good manners
to give place to the last comer,
and affect not to speak
louder than ordinary.

9

Spit not in the fire,
nor stoop low before it.
Neither put your hands
into the flames
to warm them,
nor set your feet
upon the fire,
especially if there
be meat before it.

10

When you sit down,
keep your feet firm
and even,
without putting
one on the other
or crossing them.

11

Shift not yourself
in the sight of others
nor gnaw your nails.

12

Shake not the head,
feet, or legs, roll not the eyes,
lift not one eyebrow
higher than the other,
wry not the mouth,
and bedew no man's face
with your spittle
by approaching too near
him when you speak.

13

Kill no vermin, as
fleas, lice, ticks, and company,
in the sight of others.
If you see any filth or
thick spittle put your foot
dexterously upon it,
if it be upon the clothes
of your companions
put it off privately,
and if it be upon
your own clothes
return thanks to him
who puts it off.

14

Turn not your back to others,
especially in speaking.
Jog not the table or
desk on which another
reads or writes.
Lean not upon anyone.

15

Keep your nails
clean and short,
also your hands and teeth clean,
yet without showing
any great concern for them.

16

Do not puff up the cheeks;
loll not out the tongue,
rub the hands or beard,
thrust out the lips
or bite them, or keep the lips
too open or too close.

17

Be no flatterer,
neither play with any
that delights not
to be played withal.

18

Read no letters, books,
or papers in company,
but when there is a necessity
for the doing of it
you must ask leave.
Come not near the books
or writings of another so as
to read them unless desired,
or give your opinion
of them unasked.
Also look not nigh
when another is
writing a letter.

19

Let your countenance
be pleasant but
in serious matters
somewhat grave.

20

The gestures of the body
must be suited
to the discourse you are upon.

21

Reproach none
for the infirmities of nature,
nor delight to put them
that have in mind thereof.

22

Show not yourself glad
at the misfortune
of another though
he were your enemy.

23

When you see a crime punished
you may be inwardly pleased,
but always show pity
to the suffering offender.

Darley.

24

Do not laugh too loud
or too much
at any public spectacle.

25

Superfluous complements
and all affectation of ceremony
are to be avoided,
yet where due they
are not to be neglected.

26

In pulling off your hat to persons
of distinction, as noblemen,
justices, churchmen, and company,
make a reverence, bowing more
or less according to the custom
of the better bred, and quality
of the person. Amongst your
equals expect not always that they
should begin with you first, but to
pull off the hat when there is no
need is affectation. In the
manner of saluting and
resaluting in words, keep to
the most usual custom.

27

'Tis ill manners to bid one more eminent than yourself be covered, as well as not to do it to whom it is due. Likewise, he that makes too much haste to put on his hat does not well, yet he ought to put it on at the first, or at most the second time of being asked. Now what is herein spoken, of qualification in behavior in saluting, ought also to be observed in taking of place and sitting down, for ceremonies without bounds are troublesome.

28

If anyone comes to speak
to you while you are are sitting,
stand up though he be your inferior,
and when you present seats
let it be to everyone according
to his degree.

29

When you meet with one
of greater quality than yourself,
stop and retire, especially
if it be at a door
or any straight place,
to give way for him to pass.

30

In walking, the highest place
in most countries seems
to be on the right hand,
therefore place yourself
on the left of him whom
you desire to honor.
But if three walk together
the middest place is the
most honorable. The wall
is usually given
to the most worthy
if two walk together.

31

If anyone far surpasses others,
either in age, estate, or merit,
yet would give place to a meaner
than himself in his own lodging
or elsewhere, the one ought not to
except it. So he, on the other part,
should not use much earnestness
nor offer it above once or twice.

32

To one that is your equal,
or not much inferior,
you are to give the chief place
in your lodging;
and he to who 'tis offered ought
at the first to refuse it but
at the second to accept,
though not without
acknowledging his own
unworthiness.

33

They that are in dignity
or in office have in all places
precedency, but whilst
they are young they ought
to respect those that are
their equals
in birth or other qualities,
though they have
no public charge.

34

It is good manners
to prefer them to whom
we speak before ourselves,
especially if they be above us
with whom in no sort
we ought to begin.

35

Let your discourse
with men of business
be short and comprehensive.

36

Artificers and persons
of low degree ought not
to use many ceremonies to lords
or others of high degree,
but respect and highly honor them,
and those of high degree
ought to treat them
with affability and courtesy,
without arrogancy.

37

In speaking to men of quality
do not lean nor look them full
in the face, nor approach
too near them.
At least keep a full pace
from them.

38

In visiting the sick,
do not presently play
the physician if you be
not knowing therein.

39

In writing or speaking,
give to every person
his due title according
to his degree and
the custom of the place.

40

Strive not with your superiors
in argument, but always submit
your judgment to others
with modesty.

41

Undertake not to teach
your equal in the art
himself professes;
it savours of arrogancy.

42

Let thy ceremonies in courtesy
be proper to the dignity
of his place with whom
you converse, for it is absurd
to act the same with a clown
and a prince.

43

Do not express joy
before one sick or in pain,
for that contrary passion
will aggravate his misery.

44

When a man does all he can
though it succeeds not well
blame not him that did it.

45

Being to advise or reprehend
anyone, consider whether
it ought to be in public
or in private, presently
or at some other time,
in what terms to do it;
and in reproving
show no sign of choler,
but do it with all sweetness
and mildness.

46

Take all admonitions
thankfully
in what time or place
soever given, but afterwards
not being culpable take a time
and place convenient
to let him know it
that gave them.

47

Mock not nor jest at anything
of importance, break no jests
that are sharp, biting,
and if you deliver
anything witty and pleasant,
abstain from laughing
thereat yourself.

48

Wherein you reprove another
be unblameable yourself,
for example is more prevalent
than precepts.

49

Use no reproachful language
against anyone,
neither curse nor revile.

50

Be not hasty to believe
flying reports
to the disparagement of any.

51

Wear not your clothes
foul, ripped, or dusty,
but see they be brushed
once every day at least and take
heed that you approach not
to any uncleanness.

52

In your apparel be modest
and endeavor
to accommodate nature,
rather than to procure admiration.
Keep to the fashion
of your equals,
such as are civil and
orderly with respect to times
and places.

53

Run not in the streets,
neither go too slowly
nor with mouth open.
Go not shaking your arms,
kick not the earth with
your feet,
go not upon the toes,
nor in a dancing fashion.

54

Play not the peacock,
looking everywhere about you
to see if you be well decked,
if your shoes fit well,
if your stockings sit neatly,
and clothes handsomely.

55

Eat not in the streets,
nor in the house,
out of season.

56

Associate yourself
with men of good quality
if you esteem
your own reputation;
for 'tis better to be alone
than in bad company.

57

In walking up and down in
a house, only with one in
company, if he be greater
than yourself, at the first give
him the right hand and stop not
till he does and be not the first
that turns, and when you
do turn let it be with your face
towards him. If he be a man
of great quality, walk not
with him cheek by jowl
but somewhat behind him;
but yet in such a manner
that he may easily speak to you.

58

Let your conversation
be without malice or envy,
for 'tis a sign of a tractable
and commendable nature,
and in all causes of passion
admit reason to govern.

59

Never express
anything unbecoming,
nor act against the rules
moral before your inferiors.

60

Be not immodest
in urging your friends
to discover a secret.

61

Utter not base and
frivolous things amongst
grave and learned men,
nor very difficult questions
or subjects among the ignorant,
or things hard to be believed.
Stuff not your discourse
with sentences amongst
your betters nor equals.

62

Speak not of doleful things
in a time of mirth or at
the table; speak not of
melancholy things
as death and wounds,
and if others mention them
change if you can
the discourse.
Tell not your dreams,
but to your intimate friend.

63

A man ought not to value
himself of his achievements
or rare qualities of wit,
much less of his riches,
virtue, or kindred.

64

Break not a jest
where none take pleasure
in mirth; laugh not aloud
nor at all without occasion;
deride no man's misfortune,
though there seem
to be some cause.

65

Speak not injurious words
neither in jest nor earnest;
scoff at none although
they give occasion.

66

Be not forward but friendly
and courteous, the first
to salute, hear, and answer.
Be not pensive when
it's a time to converse.

67

Detract not from others,
neither be excessive
in commanding.

68

Go not thither,
where you know not
whether you shall
be welcome or not.
Give not advice
without being asked,
and when desired do it briefly.

69

If two contend together
take not the part of either
unconstrained,
and be not obstinate
in your own opinion.
In things indifferent
be of the major side.

70

Reprehend not
the imperfections
of others, for that belongs
to parents, masters,
and superiors.

71

Gaze not on the marks
or blemishes of others
and ask not how they came.
What you may speak in secret
to your friend deliver
not before others.

72

Speak not in an unknown tongue
in company but in
your own language and
that as those of quality do
and not as the vulgar.
Sublime matters treat seriously.

73

Think before you speak,
pronounce not imperfectly
nor bring out your words
too hastily,
but orderly and distinctly.

74

When another speaks
be attentive yourself,
and disturb not the audience.
If any hesitate in his words,
help him not nor prompt him
without desired.
Interrupt him not,
nor answer him
till his speech
be ended.

75

In the midst of discourse
ask not of what one treats,
but if you perceive any stop
because of your coming
you may well entreat him
gently to proceed. If a person
of quality comes in while you're
conversing, it's handsome
to repeat what was
said before.

76

While you are talking,
point not with your finger
at him of whom you discourse,
nor approach too near him
to whom you talk,
especially to his face.

77

Treat with men at fit times
about business and
whisper not in the company
of others.

78

Make no comparisons
and if any of the company
be commended for any
brave act of virtue, commend
not another for the same.

79

Be not apt to relate news
if you know not the truth thereof.
In discoursing of things
you have heard
name not your author;
always a secret discover not.

80

Be not tedious in discourse
or in reading unless you find
the company pleased therewith.

81

Be not curious
to know the affairs of others,
neither approach those
that speak in private.

82

Undertake not
what you cannot perform
but be careful
to keep your promise.

83

When you deliver a matter
do it without passion
and with discretion,
however mean the person be
you do it to.

84

When your superiors
talk to anybody hearken not,
neither speak nor laugh.

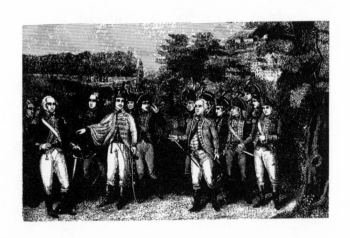

85

In company of those
of higher quality than yourself,
speak not till you are
asked a question,
then stand upright,
put off your hat,
and answer in few words.

86

In disputes, be not
so desirous to overcome
as not to give liberty
to each one
to deliver his opinion
and submit to the judgment
of the major part,
especially if there are
judges of the dispute.

87

Let thy carriage
be such as becomes a man:
grave, settled, and attentive
to that which is spoken.
Contradict not at every turn
what others say.

88

Be not tedious in discourse,
make not many digressions,
nor repeat often the
same manner
of discourse.

89

Speak not evil of the absent
for it is unjust.

90

Being set at meat
scratch not, neither spit,
cough, or blow your nose
except if there is
a necessity for it.

91

Make no show of taking
great delight in your victuals.
Feed not with greediness,
eat your bread with a knife,
lean not on the table,
neither find fault
with what you eat.

92

Take no salt or
cut bread with your knife greasy.

93

Entertaining anyone at table
it is decent to present
him with meat.
Undertake not to help others
undesired by the master.

94

If you soak bread in the sauce,
let it be no more than
what you put in your mouth
at a time, and blow not
your broth at table
but stay till it cools of itself.

95

Put not your meat to your mouth
with your knife in your hand,
neither spit forth the stones
of any fruit pie upon a dish
nor cast anything under the table.

96

It's unbecoming
to stoop much to one's meat.
Keep your fingers clean,
and when foul wipe them
on a corner of your table napkin.

97

Put not another bite
into your mouth till
the former be swallowed.
Let not your morsels
be too big for the jowls.

98

Drink not nor talk
with your mouth full,
neither gaze about you
while you are drinking.

99

Drink not too leisurely
nor yet too hastily.
Before and after drinking
wipe your lips;
breathe not then or ever
with too great a noise,
for it is uncivil.

100

Cleanse not your teeth
with the table cloth napkin,
fork, or knife, but if others do it
let it be done with a pick tooth.

101

Rinse not your mouth
in the presence of others.

102

It is out of use
to call upon the company
often to eat, nor need
you drink to others
every time you drink.

103

In company of your betters
be not longer in eating
than they are.
Lay not your arm
but only your hand
upon the table.

104

It belongs to the chiefest
in company to unfold his napkin
and fall to meat first,
but he ought then to begin
in time and to dispatch
with dexterity that the slowest
may have time allowed him.

105

Be not angry at table
whatever happens and if
you have reason to be so,
show it not but on
a cheerful countenance,
especially if there be strangers,
for good humor makes
one dish of meat a feast.

106

Set not yourself
at the upper of the table
but if it be your due
or that the master
of the house
will have it so;
contend not,
lest you should
trouble the company.

107

If others talk at table
be attentive, but talk not
with meat in your mouth.

108

When you speak
of God or His attributes,
let it be seriously and
with reverence.
Honor and obey your natural
parents although they be poor.

109

Let your recreations
be manful
not sinful.

110

Labor to keep alive
in your breast that little spark
of celestial fire
called conscience.

My station is new; and, if I may use the expression, I walk on untrodden ground. There is scarcely any part of my conduct which may not hereafter be drawn into precedent.

—IN A LETTER TO CATHERINE MACAULAY GRAHAM,

JANUARY 9, 1790

...I have the consolation to believe, that while choice and prudence invite me to quit the political scene, patriotism does not forbid it.

— ADDRESS AT THE END OF HIS PRESIDENCY, NEW YORK CITY, SEPTEMBER 19, 1796

Farewell to the Armies

GENERAL WASHINGTON'S FAREWELL ORDERS ISSUED TO THE ARMIES OF THE UNITED STATES OF AMERICA, NOVEMBER 2, 1783— ROCKY HILL, NEW JERSEY

T HE UNITED STATES IN CONGRESS assembled, after giving the most honorable testimony to the merits of the federal armies, and presenting them with the thanks of their country for their long, eminent, and faithful services, having thought proper, by their proclamation bearing date the eighteenth day of

October last, to discharge such part of the troops as were engaged for the war, and to permit the officers on furlough to retire from service from and after tomorrow, which proclamation having been communicated in the public papers for the information and government of all concerned. It only remains for the Commander in Chief to address himself once more, and that for the last time, to the armies of the United States (however widely dispersed the individuals who composed them may be) and to bid them an affectionate— a long farewell.

But before the Commander in Chief takes his final leave of those he holds most dear, he wishes to indulge himself a few moments in calling to mind a slight review of the past. He will then take the liberty of exploring with his military friends their future prospects, of advising the general line of conduct which in his opinion ought to be perused, and he will conclude the address by expressing the obligations he feels himself under for the spirited and able assistance he has experienced from them, in the performance of an arduous office.

A contemplation of the complete attainment (at a period earlier than could have been expected) of the object for which we contended, against so formidable a power, cannot but inspire us with astonishment and gratitude. The disadvantageous circumstances on our part, under which the war was undertaken, can never be forgotten. The singular interpositions of Providence in our feeble condition were such, as could scarcely escape the attention of the most unobserving—where the unparalleled perseverance of the armies of the United States, through almost every possible suffering and discouragement, for the space of eight long years was little short of a standing miracle.

It is not the meaning nor within the compass of this address, to detail the hardships peculiarly incident to our service, or to describe the distresses which in several instances have resulted from the extremes of hunger and nakedness, combined with the rigors of an inclement season. Nor is it necessary to dwell on the dark side of our past affairs. Every American officer and soldier must now console himself for any unpleasant circumstances which may have occurred, by a recollection of the uncommon scenes in which he has been called to act, no inglorious part; and the astonishing events of which he has been a witness—events which have seldom, if ever before, taken place on the stage of human action, nor can they probably ever happen again. For who has before seen a disciplined army formed at once from such raw materials? Who that was not a witness could imagine, that the most violent local prejudices would cease so soon, and that men who came from the different parts of the continent, strongly disposed by the habits of education, to despise and quarrel with each other, would instantly become but one patriotic band of brothers? Or who that was not on the spot can trace the steps by which such a wonderful revolution has been affected, and such a glorious period put to all our warlike toils?

It is universally acknowledged that the enlarged prospect of happiness, opened by the confirmation of our independence and sovereignty, almost exceeds the power of description. And shall not the brave men who have contributed so essentially to these inestimable acquisitions, retiring victorious from the field of war to the field of agriculture, participate in all the blessings which have been obtained? In such a republic, who will exclude them from the rights of citizens and the fruits of their labors? In such a country so happily circumstanced the pursuits of commerce and the cultivation of the soil, will unfold to industry the certain road to competence. To those hardy soldiers, who are actuated by the spirit of adventure, the fisheries will afford ample and profitable employment, and the extensive and fertile regions of the west will yield a most happy asylum to those, who, fond of domestic enjoyment, are seeking for personal independence. Nor is it possible to conceive that anyone of the United States will prefer a national bankruptcy and a dissolution of the union, to a compliance with the requisitions of Congress and the payment of its just debts—so that the officers and soldiers may expect considerable assistance in recommencing their civil occupations from the sums due to them from the public, which must and will most inevitably be paid.

In order to effect this desirable purpose, and to remove the prejudices which may have taken possession of the minds of any of the good people of the States, it is earnestly recommended to all the troops that with strong attachments to the Union, they should carry with them into civil society the most conciliating dispositions; and that they should prove themselves not less virtuous and useful as citizens, than they have been persevering and victorious as soldiers. What though there should be some envious individuals who are unwilling to pay the debt the public has contracted, or to yield the tribute due to merit, yet let such unworthy treatment produce no invective, or any instance of intemperate conduct, let it be remembered that the unbiased voice of the free citizens of the United States has promised the just reward, and given the merited applause, let it be known and remembered that the reputation of the federal armies is established beyond the reach of malevolence, and let a consciousness of their achievements and fame, still incite the men who composed them to honorable actions; under the persuasion that the private virtues of economy, prudence and industry, will not be less amiable in civil life, than the more splendid qualities of valor, perseverance and enterprise, were in the field. Everyone may rest assured that much, very much of the future happiness of the officers and men, will depend upon the wise and manly conduct which shall be adopted by them, when they are mingled with the great body of the community. And although the General has so frequently given it as his opinion in the most public and explicit manner, that unless the principles of the federal government were properly supported, and the powers of the union increased, the honor, dignity, and justice of the nation would be lost forever; yet he cannot help repeating on this occasion, so interesting a sentiment, and leaving it as his last injunction to every officer and every soldier, who may view the subject in the same serious point of light, to add his best endeavors to those of his worthy fellow citizens towards effecting these great and valuable purposes, on which our very existence as a nation so materially depends.

The Commander in Chief conceives little is now waiting to enable the soldier to change the military character into that of the citizen but that steady and decent tenor of behavior which has generally distinguished, not only the army under his immediate command, but the different detachments and separate armies, through the course of the war; from their good sense and prudence he anticipates the happiest consequences; and while he congratulates them on the glorious occasion which renders their services in the field no longer necessary, he wishes to express the strong obligations he feels himself under, for the assistance he has received from every class— and in every instance. He presents his thanks in the most serious and affectionate manner to the general officers, as well for their counsel on many interesting occasions, as for their ardor in promoting the success of the plans he had adopted. To the Commandants of Regiments and Corps, and to the other officers for their great zeal and attention in carrying his orders promptly into execution. To the Staff for their alacrity and exactness in performing the duties of their several departments. And to the non-commissioned officers and private soldiers, for their extraordinary patience in suffering, as well as their invincible fortitude in action. To the various branches of the army, the General takes this last and solemn opportunity of professing his inviolable attachment and friendship. He wishes more than bare professions were in his power, that he was really able to be useful to them all in future life; he flatters himself, however, they will do him the justice to believe, that whatever could with propriety be attempted by him has been done. And being now to conclude these his last public orders, to take his ultimate leave, in a short time, of the military character, and to bid a final adieu to the armies he has so long had the honor to command—he can only again offer in their behalf his recommendations to their grateful country, and his prayers to the god of armies. May ample justice be done them here, and may the choicest of heaven's favors both here and hereafter attend those, who under the divine auspices have secured innumerable blessings for others. With these wishes, and this benediction, the Commander in Chief is about to retire from service. The curtain of separation will soon be drawn, and the military scene to him will be closed forever.

Upon the decease of my wife, it is my will and desire that all the slaves which I hold in my own right, shall receive their freedom....And whereas among those who will receive freedom according to this devise, there may be some, who from old age or bodily infirmities, and others who on account of their infancy, that will be unable to support themselves; it is my will and desire that all who come under the first and second description shall be comfortably clothed and fed by my heirs while they live...

—From George Washington's
Last Will and Testament,
Mount Vernon, July 9, 1799

Army Retirement Address
TO THE CONTINENTAL CONGRESS, DECEMBER 23, 1783— ANNAPOLIS, MARYLAND

MR PRESIDENT:

The great events on which my resignation depended having at length taken place; I have now the honor of offering my sincere congratulations to Congress and of presenting myself before them to surrender into their hands the trust committed to me, and to claim the indulgence of retiring from the service of my country.

Happy in the confirmation of our independence and sovereignty, and pleased with the opportunity afforded the United States of becoming a respectable nation, I resign with satisfaction the appointment I accepted with diffidence—a diffidence in my abilities to accomplish so arduous a task, which however was superseded by a confidence in the rectitude of our cause, the support of the supreme power of the union, and the patronage of heaven.

The successful termination of the war has verified the more sanguine expectations, and my gratitude for the interposition of Providence, and the assistance I have received from my countrymen increases with every review of the momentous contest.

While I repeat my obligations to the army in general, I should do injustice to my own feelings not to acknowledge in this place the peculiar services and distinguished merits of the gentlemen who have been attached to my person during the war. It was impossible the choice of confidential officers to compose my family should have been more fortunate.

Permit me, sir, to recommend in particular those who have continued in service to the present moment as worthy of the favorable notice and patronage of Congress.

I consider it an indispensable duty to close this last solemn act of my official life by commanding the interests of our dearest country to the protection of almighty God, and those who have the superintendence of them, to his holy keeping.

Having now finished the work assigned me, I retire from the great theater of action—and bidding an affectionate farewell to this august body under whose orders I have so long acted, I here offer my commission, and take my leave of all the employments of public life.

The General is sorry to be informed that the foolish, and wicked practice, of profane cursing and swearing (a vice heretofore little known in an American army) is growing into fashion; he hopes the officers will, by example, as well as influence, endeavor to check it, and that both they, and the men will reflect, that we can have little hopes of the blessing of heaven on our arms, if we insult it by our impiety, and folly; added to this, it is a vice so mean and low, without any temptation, that every man of sense, and character, detests and despises it.

—IN A LETTER FROM HEADQUARTERS TO THE ARMY, NEW YORK, AUGUST 3, 1776

Washington's First Inaugural Address

APRIL 30, 1789—

NEW YORK CITY

❧

FELLOW CITIZENS OF THE SENATE AND THE House of Representatives.

Among the vicissitudes incident to life, no event could have filled me with greater anxieties than that of which the notification was transmitted by your order, and received on the fourteenth day of the present month. On the one hand, I was summoned by my country, whose voice I can never hear but with veneration and love, from a retreat which I had chosen with the fondest predilection, and, in my flattering hopes, with an immutable decision, as the asylum of my declining years: a retreat which was rendered every day more necessary as well as more dear to me, by the addition of habit to inclination, and of frequent interruptions in my health to the gradual waste committed on it by time. On the other hand, the magnitude and difficulty of the trust to which the voice of my country called me, being sufficient to awaken in the wisest and most experienced of her citizens, a distrustful scrutiny into his qualifications, could not but overwhelm with despondence, one, who, inheriting inferior endowments from nature and unpracticed in the duties of civil administration, ought to be peculiarly conscious of his own deficiencies. In this conflict of emotions, all I dare aver, is that it has been my faithful study to collect my duty from a just appreciation of every circumstance by which it might be affected. All I dare hope, is, that, if in executing this task I have been too much swayed by a grateful remembrance of former instances, or by an affectionate sensibility to this transcendent proof, of the confidence of my fellow-citizens; and have thence too little consulted my incapacity as well as disinclination for the weighty and untried cares before me; my error will be palliated by the motives which misled me, and its consequences be judged by my country, with some share of the partiality in which they originated.

Such being the impressions under which I have, in obedience to the public summons, repaired to the present station; it would be peculiarly improper to omit in this first official act, my fervent supplications to that almighty being who rules over the universe, who presides in the councils of nations, and whose providential aids can supply every human defect, that his benediction may consecrate to the liberties and happiness of the people of the United States, a government instituted by themselves for these essential purposes and may enable every instrument employed in its administration to execute with success, the functions allotted to his charge. In tendering this homage to the great author of every public and private good I assure myself that it expresses your sentiments not less than my own; nor those of my fellow-citizens at large, less than either. No people can be bound to acknowledge and adore the invisible hand which conducts the affairs of men more than the people of the United States. Every step, by which they have advanced to the character of an independent nation, seems to have been distinguished by some token of providential agency. And in the important revolution just accomplished in the system of their united government, the tranquil deliberations and voluntary consent of so many distinct communities from which the event has resulted, cannot be compared with the means by which most governments have been established, without some return of pious gratitude along with an humble anticipation of the future blessings which the past seem to presage. These reflections, arising out of the present crisis, have forced themselves too strongly on my mind to be suppressed. You will join with me I trust in thinking, that there are none under the influence of which the proceedings of a new and free government can more auspiciously commence.

By the article establishing the executive department, it is made the duty of the President "to recommend to your consideration, such measures as he shall judge necessary and expedient." The circumstances under which I now meet you, will acquit me from entering into that subject, farther than to refer to the great constitutional charter under which you are assembled; and which, in defining your powers, designates the objects to which your attention is to be given. It will be more consistent with those circumstances, and far more congenial with the feelings which actuate me, to substitute, in place of a recommendation of particular measures, the tribute that is due to the talents, the rectitude, and the patriotism which adorn the characters selected to devise and adopt them. In these honorable qualifications, I behold the surest pledges, that as on one side, no local prejudices, or attachments, no separate views, nor party animosities, will misdirect the comprehensive and equal eye which ought to watch over this great assemblage of communities and interests; so, on another, that the foundations of our national policy will be laid in the pure and immutable principles of private morality; and the pre-eminence of a free government, be exemplified by all the attributes which can win the affections of its citizens, and command the respect of the world.

I dwell on this prospect with every satisfaction which an ardent love for my country can inspire, since there is no truth more thoroughly established than that there exists in the economy and course of nature an indissoluble union between virtue and happiness, between duty and advantage, between the genuine maxims of an honest and magnanimous policy, and the solid rewards of public prosperity and felicity. Since we ought to be no less persuaded that the propitious smiles of heaven, can never be expected on a nation that disregards the eternal rules of order and right, which heaven itself has ordained; and since the preservation of the sacred fire of liberty, and the destiny of the republican model of government, are justly considered as deeply, perhaps as finally staked, on the experiment entrusted to the hands of the American people.

Besides the ordinary objects submitted to your care, it will remain with your judgment to decide, how far an exercise of the occasional power delegated by the fifth article of the Constitution is rendered expedient at the present juncture by the nature of objections which have been urged against the system, or by the degree of inquietude which has given birth to them. Instead of undertaking particular recommendations on this subject, in which I could be guided by no lights derived from official opportunities, I shall again give way to my entire confidence in your discernment and pursuit of the public good: For I assure myself that whilst you carefully avoid every alteration which might endanger the benefits of an united and effective government, or which ought to await the future lessons of experience; a reverence for the characteristic rights of freemen, and a regard for the public harmony, will sufficiently influence your deliberations on the question how far the former can be more impregnably fortified, or the latter be safely and advantageously promoted.

To the preceding observations I have one to add, which will be most properly addressed to the House of Representatives. It concerns myself, and will therefore be as brief as possible. When I was first honored with a call into the service of my country, then on the eve of an arduous struggle for its liberties, the light in which I contemplated my duty required that I should renounce every pecuniary compensation. From this resolution I have in no instance departed. And being still under the impressions which produced it, I must decline as inapplicable to myself, any share in the personal emoluments, which may be indispensably included in a permanent provision for the executive department; and must accordingly pray that the pecuniary estimates for the station in which I am placed, may, during my continuance in it, be limited to such actual expenditures as the public good may be thought to require.

Having thus imported to you my sentiments, as they have been awakened by the occasion which brings us together, I shall take my present leave; but not without resorting once more to the benign parent of the human race, in humble supplication that since he has been pleased to favor the American people, with opportunities for deliberating in perfect tranquility, and dispositions for deciding with unparalleled unanimity on a form of government, for the security of their union, and the advancement of their happiness; so his divine blessing may be equally *conspicuous* in the enlarged views, the temperate consultations, and the wise measures on which the success of this government must depend.

Address at the End of His Presidency

SEPTEMBER 19, 1796—
FIRST PUBLISHED IN
PHILADELPHIA

FRIENDS AND FELLOW CITIZENS:

The period for a new election of a citizen to administer the executive government of the United States, being not far distant, and the time actually arrived, when your thoughts must be employed in designating the person, who is to be clothed with that important trust, it appears to me proper, especially as it may conduce to a more distinct expression of the public voice, that I should now apprise you of the resolution I have formed, to decline being considered among the number of those, out of whom a choice is to be made.

I beg you, at the same time, to do me the justice to be assured, that this resolution has not been taken, without a strict regard to all the considerations appertaining to the relation, which binds a dutiful citizen to his country—and that, in withdrawing the tender of service which silence in my situation might imply, I am influenced by no diminution of zeal for your future interest, no deficiency of grateful respect for your past kindness; but am supported by a full conviction that the step is compatible with both.

The acceptance of, and continuance hitherto in, the office to which your suffrages have twice called me, have been a uniform sacrifice of inclination to the opinion of duty, and to a deference for what appeared to be your desire. I constantly hoped, that it would have been much earlier in my power, consistently with motives, which I was not at liberty to disregard, to return to that retirement, from which I had been reluctantly drawn. The strength of my inclination to do this, previous to the last election, had even led to the preparation of an address to declare it to you; but mature reflection on the then perplexed and critical posture of our affairs with foreign nations, and the unanimous advice of persons entitled to my confidence, impelled me to abandon the idea.

I rejoice, that the state of your concerns, external as well as internal, no longer renders the pursuit of inclination incompatible with the sentiment of duty, or propriety; and am persuaded whatever partiality may be retained for my services, that in the present circumstances of our country, you will not disapprove my determination to retire.

The impressions with which I first undertook the arduous trust were explained on the proper occasion. In the discharge of this trust, I will only say, that I have, with good intentions, contributed towards the organization and administration of the government, the best exertions of which a very fallible judgment was capable. Not unconscious, in the outset, of the inferiority of my qualifications, experience in my own eyes, perhaps still more in the eyes of others, has strengthened the motives to diffidence of myself; and every day the increasing weight of years admonishes me more and more, that the shade of retirement is as necessary to me as it will be welcome. Satisfied that if any circumstances have given peculiar value to my services, they were temporary, I have the consolation to believe, that while choice and prudence invite me to quit the political scene, patriotism does not forbid it.

In looking forward to the moment, which is intended to terminate the career of my public life, my feelings do not permit me to suspend the deep acknowledgment of that debt of gratitude which I owe to my beloved country, for the many honors it has conferred upon me; still more for the steadfast confidence with which it has supported me; and for the opportunities I have thence enjoyed of manifesting my inviolable attachment, by services faithful and persevering, though in usefulness unequal to my zeal. If benefits have resulted to our country from these services, let it always be remembered to your praise, and as an instructive example in our annals, that, under circumstances in which the passions agitated in every direction were liable to mislead, amidst appearances sometimes dubious, vicissitudes of fortune often discouraging, in situations in which not infrequently want of success has countenanced the spirit of criticism, the constancy of your support was the essential prop of the efforts, and a guarantee of the plans by which they were effected. Profoundly penetrated with this idea, I shall carry it with me to my grave, as a strong incitement to unceasing vows that heaven may continue to you the choicest tokens of its beneficence—that your union and brotherly affection may be perpetual—that the free constitution, which is the work of your hands, may be sacredly maintained—that its administration in every department may be stamped with wisdom and virtue—that, in fine, the happiness of the people of these States, under the auspices of liberty, may be made complete, by so careful a preservation and so prudent a use of this blessing as will acquire to them the glory of recommending it to the applause, the affection—and adoption of every nation which is yet a stranger to it.

Here, perhaps, I ought to stop. But a solicitude for your welfare, which cannot end but with my life, and the apprehension of danger, natural to that solicitude, urge me on an occasion like the present, to offer to your solemn contemplation, and to recommend to your frequent review, some sentiments; which are the result of much reflection, of no inconsiderable observation, and which appear to me all important to the permanency of your felicity as a people. These will be offered to you with the more freedom as you can only see in them the disinterested warnings of a parting friend, who can possibly have no personal motive to bias his counsel. Nor can I forget, as an encouragement to it, your indulgent reception of my sentiments on a former and not dissimilar occasion.

Interwoven as is the love of liberty with every ligament of your hearts, no recommendation of mine is necessary to fortify or confirm the attachment.

The unity of government which constitutes you one people is also now dear to you. It is justly so; for it is a main pillar in the edifice of your real independence, the support of your tranquility at home; your peace abroad; of your safety; of your prosperity; of that very liberty which you so highly prize. But as it is easy to foresee, that from different causes and from different quarters, much pains will be taken, many artifices employed, to weaken in your minds the conviction of this truth; as this is the point in your political fortress against which the batteries of internal and external enemies will be most constantly and actively (though often covertly and insidiously) directed, it is of infinite moment that you should properly estimate the immense value of your national union to your collective and individual happiness; that you should cherish a cordial, habitual, and immovable attachment to it; accustoming yourselves to think and speak of it as of the palladium of your political safety and prosperity; watching for its preservation with jealous anxiety; discountenancing whatever may suggest even a suspicion that it can in any event be abandoned, and indignantly frowning upon the first dawning of every attempt to alienate any portion of our country from the rest, or to enfeeble the sacred ties which now link together the various parts.

For this you have every inducement of sympathy and interest. Citizens by birth or choice, of a common country, that country has a right to concentrate your affections. The name of American, which belongs to you, in your national capacity, must always exalt the just pride of patriotism, more than any appellation derived from local discriminations.

With slight shades of difference, you have the same religion, manners, habits, and political principles. You have in a common cause fought and triumphed together—the independence and liberty you possess are the work of joint councils, and joint efforts, of common dangers, sufferings, and successes.

But these considerations, however powerfully they address themselves to your sensibility are greatly outweighed by those which apply more immediately to your interest. Here every portion of our country finds the most commanding motives for carefully guarding and preserving the union of the whole.

The North, in an unrestrained intercourse with the South, protected by the equal laws of a common government, finds in the productions of the latter, great additional resources of maritime and commercial enterprise and precious materials of manufacturing industry. The South in the same intercourse, benefiting by the agency of the North, sees its agriculture grow and its commerce expand. Turning partly into its own channels the seamen of the North, it finds its particular navigation invigorated; and while it contributes, in different ways, to nourish and increase the general mass of the national navigation, it looks forward to the protection of a maritime strength, to which itself is unequally adapted. The East, in a like intercourse with the West, already finds, and in the progressive improvement of interior communications by land and water, will more and more find a valuable vent for the commodities which it brings from abroad, or manufactures at home. The West derives from the East supplies requisite to its growth and comfort—and what is perhaps of still greater consequence, it must of necessity owe the secure enjoyment of indispensable outlets for its own productions to the weight, influence, and the future maritime strength of the atlantic side of the union, directed by an indissoluble community of interest as one nation. Any other tenure by which the West can hold this essential advantage, whether derived from its own separate strength, or from an apostate and unnatural connection with any foreign power, must be intrinsically precarious.

While then every part of our country thus feels an immediate and particular interest in union, all the parts combined cannot fail to find in the united mass of means and efforts greater strength, greater resource, proportionally greater security from external danger, a less frequent interruption of their peace by foreign nations; and, what is of inestimable value they must derive from union an exemption from those broils and wars between themselves, which so frequently afflict neighboring countries, not tied together by the same government; which their own rivalships alone would be sufficient to produce, but which opposite foreign alliances, attachments, and intrigues would stimulate and embitter. Hence likewise they will avoid the necessity of those overgrown military establishments, which under any form of government are inauspicious to liberty, and which are to be regarded as particularly hostile to republican liberty. In this sense it is, that your union ought to be considered as a main prop of your liberty, and that the love of the one ought to endear to you the preservation of the other.

These considerations speak a persuasive language to every reflecting and virtuous mind, and exhibit the continuance of the union as a primary object of patriotic desire. Is there a doubt, whether a common government can embrace so large a sphere? Let experience solve it. To listen to mere speculation in such a case were criminal. We are authorized to hope that a proper organization of the whole, with the auxiliary agency of governments for the respective subdivisions, will afford a happy issue to the experiment. 'Tis well worth a fair and full experiment.

With such powerful and obvious motives to union, affecting all parts of our country, while experience shall not have demonstrated its impracticability, there will always be reason to distrust the patriotism of those who in any quarter may endeavor to weaken its bands.

In contemplating the causes which may disturb our union, it occurs as matter of serious concern, that any ground should have been furnished for characterizing parties by geographical discriminations—northern and southern, atlantic and western—whence designing men may endeavor to excite a belief that there is a real difference of local interests and views.

One of the expedients of party to acquire influence, within particular districts, is to misrepresent the opinions and aims of other districts. You cannot shield yourselves too much against the jealousies and heart burnings which spring from these misrepresentations. They tend to render alien to each other those who ought to be bound together by fraternal affection. The inhabitants of our western country have lately had a useful lesson on this head. They have seen, in the negotiation by the executive, and in the unanimous ratification by the senate, of the treaty with Spain, and in the universal satisfaction at that event, throughout the United States, a decisive proof how unfounded were the suspicions propagated among them of a policy in the general government and in the atlantic states unfriendly to their interests in regard to the Mississippi. They have been witnesses to the formation of two treaties, that with Great Britain and that with Spain, which secure to them every thing they could desire, in respect to our foreign relations, towards confirming their prosperity. Will it not be their wisdom to rely for the preservation of these advantages on the union by which they were procured? Will they not henceforth be deaf to those advisers, if such there are, who would sever them from their brethren and connect them with aliens?

To the efficacy and permanency of your union, a government for the whole is indispensable. No alliances however strict between the parts can be an adequate substitute. They must inevitably experience the infractions and interruptions which all alliances in all times have experienced. Sensible of this momentous truth, you have improved upon your first essay, by the adoption of a Constitution of government, better calculated than your former for an intimate union, and for the efficacious management of your common concerns. This government, the offspring of our own choice uninfluenced and unawed, adopted upon full investigation and mature deliberation, completely free in its principles, in the distribution of its powers, uniting security with energy, and containing within itself a provision for its own amendment, has a just claim to your confidence and your support. respect for its authority, compliance with its laws, acquiescence in its measures, are duties enjoined by the fundamental maxims of true liberty. The basis of our political systems is the right of the people to make and to alter their constitutions of government. But the Constitution which at any time exists, till changed by an explicit and authentic act of the whole people, is sacredly obligatory upon all. The very idea of the power and the right of the people to establish government presupposes the duty of every individual to obey the established government.

All obstructions to the execution of the laws, all combinations and associations, under whatever plausible character, with the real design to direct, control counteract, or awe the regular deliberation and action of the constituted authorities are destructive of this fundamental principle and of fatal tendency. They serve to organize faction, to give it an artificial and extraordinary force—to put in the place of the delegated will of the nation, the will of a party; often a small but artful and enterprising minority of the community; and, according to the alternate triumphs of different parties, to make the public administration the mirror of the ill concerted and incongruous projects of faction, rather than the organ of consistent and wholesome plans digested by common councils and modified by mutual interests. However combinations or associations of the above description may now and then answer popular ends, they are likely, in the course of time and things, to become potent engines, by which cunning, ambitious, and unprincipled men will be enabled to subvert the power of the people, and to usurp for themselves the reins of government; destroying afterwards the very engines which have lifted them to unjust dominion.

Towards the preservation of your government and the permanency of your present happy state, it is requisite, not only that you steadily discountenance irregular oppositions to its acknowledged authority, but also that you resist with care the spirit of innovation upon its principles however specious the pretexts. One method of assault may be to effect, in the forms of the Constitution, alterations which will impair the energy of the system, and thus to undermine what cannot be directly overthrown. In all the changes to which you may be invited, remember that time and habit are at least as necessary to fix the true character of governments as of other human institutions—that experience is the surest standard by which to test the real tendency of the existing constitution of a country—that facility in changes upon the credit of mere hypotheses and opinion exposes to perpetual change, from the endless variety of hypotheses and opinion; and remember, especially, that for the efficient management of your common interests, in a country so extensive as ours, a government of as much vigor as is consistent with the perfect security of liberty is indispensable. Liberty itself will find in such a government, with powers properly distributed and adjusted, its surest guardian. It is indeed little else than a name, where the government is too feeble to withstand the enterprises of faction, to confine each member of the society within the limits prescribed by the laws and to maintain all in the secure and tranquil enjoyment of the rights of person and property.

I have already intimated to you the danger of parties in the state, with particular reference to the founding of them on geographical discriminations. Let me now take a more comprehensive view, and warn you in the most solemn manner against the baneful effects of the spirit of party, generally.

This spirit, unfortunately, is inseparable from our nature, having its root in the strongest passions of the human mind. It exists under different shapes in all governments, more or less stifled, controlled, or repressed; but in those of the popular form it is seen in its greatest rankness and is truly their worst enemy.

The alternate domination of one faction over another, sharpened by the spirit of revenge natural to party dissention, which in different ages and countries has perpetrated the most horrid enormities, is itself a frightful despotism. But this leads at length to a more formal and permanent despotism. The disorders and miseries which result gradually incline the minds of men to seek security and repose in the absolute power of an individual: and sooner or later the chief of some prevailing faction more able or more fortunate than his competitors, turns this disposition to the purposes of his own elevation, on the ruins of public liberty.

Without looking forward to an extremity of this kind (which nevertheless ought not to be entirely out of sight) the common and continual mischief's of the spirit of party are sufficient to make it the interest and the duty of a wise people to discourage and restrain it.

It serves always to distract the public councils and enfeeble the public administration. It agitates the community with ill founded jealousies and false alarms, kindles the animosity of one part against another, foments occasionally riot and insurrection. It opens the door to foreign influence and corruption, which find a facilitated access to the government itself through the channels of party passions. Thus the policy and the will of one country are subjected to the policy and will of another.

There is an opinion that parties in free countries are useful checks upon the administration of the government and serve to keep alive the spirit of liberty. This within certain limits is probably true—and in governments of a monarchical cast patriotism may look with indulgence, if not with favor, upon the spirit of party. But in those of the popular character, in governments purely elective, it is a spirit not to be encouraged. From their natural tendency, it is certain there will always be enough of that spirit for every salutary purpose. And there being constant danger of excess, the effort ought to be, by force of public opinion, to mitigate and assuage it. A fire not to be quenched; it demands a uniform vigilance to prevent its bursting into a flame, lest instead of warming it should consume.

It is important, likewise, that the habits of thinking in a free country should inspire caution in those entrusted with its administration, to confine themselves within their respective constitutional spheres; avoiding in the exercise of the powers of one department to encroach upon another. The spirit of encroachment tends to consolidate the powers of all the departments in one, and thus to create whatever the form of government, a real despotism. A just estimate of that love of power, and proneness to abuse it, which predominates in the human heart, is sufficient to satisfy us of the truth of this position. The necessity of reciprocal checks in the exercise of political power by dividing and distributing it into different depositories, and constituting each the guardian of the public weal against invasions by the others, has been evinced by experiments ancient and modern; some of them in our country and under our own eyes. To preserve them must be as necessary as to institute them. If in the opinion of the people, the distribution or modification of the constitutional powers be in any particular wrong, let it be corrected by an amendment in the way which the Constitution designates. But let there be no change by usurpation; for though this, in one instance, may be the instrument of good, it is the customary weapon by which free governments are destroyed. The precedent must always greatly overbalance in permanent evil any partial or transient benefit which the use can at any time yield.

Of all the dispositions and habits which lead to political prosperity, religion and morality are indispensable supports. In vain would that man claim the tribute of patriotism who should labor to subvert these great pillars of human happiness, these firmest props of the duties of men and citizens. The mere politician equally with the pious man ought to respect and to cherish them. A volume could not trace all their connections with private and public felicity. Let it simply be asked where is the security for property, for reputation, for life, if the sense of religious obligation desert the oaths, which are the instruments of investigation in courts of justice? And let us with caution indulge the supposition, that morality can be maintained without religion. Whatever may be conceded to the influence of refined education on minds of peculiar structure—reason and experience both forbid us to expect that national morality can prevail in exclusion of religious principle.

'Tis substantially true, that virtue or morality is a necessary spring of popular government. The rule indeed extends with more or less force to every species of free government. Who that is a sincere friend to it, can look with indifference upon attempts to shake the foundation of the fabric. Promote then as an object of primary importance, institutions for the general diffusion of knowledge. In proportion as the structure of a government gives force to public opinion, it is essential that public opinion should be enlightened.

As a very important source of strength and security, cherish public credit. One method of preserving it is to use it as sparingly as possible: avoiding occasions of expense by cultivating peace, but remembering also that timely disbursements to prepare for danger frequently prevent much greater disbursements to repel it—avoiding likewise the accumulation of debt, not only by shunning occasions of expense, but by vigorous exertions in time of peace to discharge the debts which unavoidable wars may have occasioned, not ungenerously throwing upon posterity the burthen which we ourselves ought to bear. The execution of these maxims belongs to your representatives, but it is necessary that public opinion should cooperate. To facilitate to them the performance of their duty, it is essential that you should practically bear in mind, that towards the payment of debts there must be revenue—that to have revenue there must be taxes—that no taxes can be devised which are not more or less inconvenient and unpleasant—that the intrinsic embarrassment inseparable from the selection of the proper objects (which is always a choice of difficulties) ought to be a decisive motive for a candid construction of the conduct of the government in making it, and for a spirit of acquiescence in the measures for obtaining revenue which the public exigencies may at any time dictate.

Observe good faith and justice towards all nations. Cultivate peace and harmony with all—

religion and morality enjoin this conduct; and can it be that good policy does not equally enjoin it? It will be worthy of a free, enlightened, and, at no distant period, a great nation, to give to mankind the magnanimous and too novel example of a people always guided by an exalted justice and benevolence. Who can doubt that in the course of time and things the fruits of such a plan would richly repay any temporary advantages which might be lost by a steady adherence to it? Can it be, that providence has not connected the permanent felicity of a nation with its virtue? The experiment, at least, is recommended by every sentiment which ennobles human nature. Alas! is it rendered impossible by its vices?

In the execution of such a plan nothing is more essential than that permanent inveterate antipathies against particular nations and passionate attachments for others should be excluded; and that in place of them just and amicable feelings towards all should be cultivated. The nation, which indulges towards another an habitual hatred, or an habitual fondness, is in some degree a slave. It is a slave to its animosity or to its affection, either of which is sufficient to lead it astray from its duty and its interest. Antipathy in one nation against another—disposes each more readily to offer insult and injury, to lay hold of slight causes of umbrage, and to be haughty and intractable, when accidental or trifling occasions of dispute occur. Hence frequent collisions, obstinate envenomed and bloody contests. The nation, prompted by ill will and resentment, sometimes impels to war the government, contrary to the best calculations of policy. The government sometimes participates in the national propensity, and adopts through passion what reason would reject; at other times, it makes the animosity of the nation subservient to projects of hostility instigated by pride, ambition, and other sinister and pernicious motives. The peace often, sometimes perhaps the liberty, of nations has been the victim.

So likewise, a passionate attachment of one nation for another produces a variety of evils. Sympathy for the favorite nation, facilitating the illusion of an imaginary common interest, in cases where no real common interest exists, and infusing into one the enmities of the other, betrays the former into a participation in the quarrels and wars of the latter, without adequate inducement or justification. It leads also to concessions to the favorite nation of privileges denied to others, which is apt doubly to injure the nation making the concessions—by unnecessarily parting with what ought to have been retained—and by exciting jealousy, ill will, and a disposition to retaliate, in the parties from whom equal privileges are withheld; and it gives to ambitious, corrupted, or deluded citizens (who devote themselves to the favorite nation) facility to betray, or sacrifice the interests of their own country, without odium, sometimes even with popularity; gilding with the appearances of a virtuous sense of obligation a commendable deference for public opinion, or a laudable zeal for public good, the base or foolish compliances of ambition, corruption, or infatuation.

As avenues to foreign influence in innumerable ways, such attachments are particularly alarming to the truly enlightened and independent patriot. How many opportunities do they afford to tamper with domestic factions, to practice the arts of seduction, to mislead public opinion, to influence or awe the public councils! Such an attachment of a small or weak, towards a great and powerful nation, dooms the former to be the satellite of the latter.

Against the insidious wiles of foreign influence, (I conjure you to believe me fellow citizens,), the jealousy of a free people ought to be constantly awake; since history and experience prove that foreign influence is one of the most baneful foes of republican government. But that jealousy to be useful must be impartial; else it becomes the instrument of the very influence to be avoided, instead of a defense against it. Excessive partiality for one foreign nation and excessive dislike of another, cause those whom they actuate to see danger only on one side, and serve to veil and even second the arts of influence on the other. Real patriots, who may resist the intrigues of the favorite, are liable to become suspected and odious; while its tools and dupes usurp the applause and confidence of the people to surrender their interests.

The great rule of conduct for us, in regard to foreign nations is in extending our commercial relations to have with them as little political connection as possible. So far as we have already formed engagements let them be fulfilled, with perfect good faith. Here let us stop.

Europe has a set of primary interests, which to us have none, or a very remote relation. Hence she must be engaged in frequent controversies, the causes of which are essentially foreign to our concerns. Hence therefore it must be unwise in us to implicate ourselves, by artificial ties, in the ordinary vicissitudes of her politics, or the ordinary combinations and collisions of her friendships, or enmities.

Our detached and distant situation invites and enables us to pursue a different course. If we remain one people, under an efficient government, the period is not far off, when we may defy material injury from external annoyance; when we may take such an attitude as will cause the neutrality we may at any time resolve upon to be scrupulously respected; when belligerent nations, under the impossibility of making acquisitions upon us, will not lightly hazard the giving us provocation; when we may choose peace or war, as our interest guided by justice shall counsel.

Why forego the advantages of so peculiar a situation? Why quit our own to stand upon foreign ground? Why, by interweaving our destiny with that of any part of Europe, entangle our peace and prosperity in the toils of European ambition, rivalship, interest, humor, or caprice?

'Tis our true policy to steer clear of permanent alliances, with any portion of the foreign World—so far, I mean, as we are now at liberty to do it—for let me not be understood as capable of patronizing infidelity to existing engagements (I hold the maxim no less applicable to public than to private affairs, that honesty is always the best policy). I repeat it therefore, let those engagements be observed in their genuine sense. But in my opinion, it is unnecessary and would be unwise to extend them.

Taking care always to keep ourselves, by suitable establishments, on a respectably defensive posture, we may safely trust to temporary alliances for extraordinary emergencies.

Harmony, liberal intercourse with all nations, are recommended by policy, humanity and interest. But even our commercial policy should hold an equal and impartial hand: neither seeking nor granting exclusive favors or preferences; consulting the natural course of things; diffusing and diversifying by gentle means the streams of commerce, but forcing nothing; establishing with powers so disposed—in order to give to trade a stable course, to define the rights of our merchants, and to enable the government to support them—conventional rules of intercourse, the best that present circumstances and mutual opinion will permit, but temporary, and liable to be from time to time abandoned or varied, as experience and circumstances shall dictate; constantly keeping in view, that 'tis folly in one nation to look for disinterested favors from another—that it must pay with a portion of its independence for whatever it may accept under that character—that by such acceptance, it may place itself in the condition of having given equivalents for nominal favors and yet of being reproached with ingratitude for not giving more. There can be no greater error than to expect, or calculate upon real favors from nation to nation. 'Tis an illusion which experience must cure, which a just pride ought to discard.

In offering to you, my countrymen, these counsels of an old and affectionate friend, I dare not hope they will make the strong and lasting impression, I could wish—that they will control the usual current of the passions, or prevent our nation from running the course which has hitherto marked the destiny of nations. But if I may even flatter myself, that they may be productive of some partial benefit, some occasional good; that they may now and then recur to moderate the fury of party spirit, to warn against the mischief's of foreign intrigue, to guard against the impostures of pretended patriotism—this hope will be a full recompense for the solicitude for your welfare, by which they have been dictated.

How far in the discharge of my official duties, I have been guided by the principles which have been delineated, the public records and other evidences of my conduct must witness to you and to the world. To myself, the assurance of my own conscience is, that I have at least believed myself to be guided by them.

In relation to the still subsisting war in Europe, my proclamation of the 22d of April 1793 is the index to my plan. Sanctioned by your approving voice and by that of your representatives in both houses of Congress, the spirit of that measure has continually governed me; uninfluenced by any attempts to deter or divert me from it.

After deliberate examination with the aid of the best lights I could obtain I was well satisfied that our country, under all the circumstances of the case, had a right to take, and was bound in duty and interest, to take a neutral position. Having taken it, I determined, as far as should depend upon me, to maintain it, with moderation, perseverance, and firmness.

The considerations, which respect the right to hold this conduct, it is not necessary on this occasion to detail. I will only observe, that according

Nothing short of independence, it appears to me, can possibly do. A peace on other terms would, if I may be allowed the expression, be a peace of war.

— IN A LETTER TO JOHN BANISTER,

APRIL 21, 1778

defects not to think it probable that I may have committed many errors. Whatever they may be I fervently beseech the Almighty to avert or mitigate the evils to which they may tend. I shall also carry with me the hope that my country will never cease to view them with indulgence; and that after forty five years of my life dedicated to its service, with an upright zeal, the faults of incompetent abilities will be consigned to oblivion, as myself must soon be to the mansions of rest.

Relying on its kindness in this as in other things, and actuated by that fervent love towards it, which is so natural to a man, who views in it the native soil of himself and his progenitors for several generations; I anticipate with pleasing expectation that retreat, in which I promise myself to realize, without alloy, the sweet enjoyment of partaking, in the midst of my fellow citizens, the benign influence of good laws under a free government—the ever favorite object of my heart, and the happy reward, as I trust, of our mutual cares, labors, and dangers.

to my understanding of the matter, that right, so far from being denied by any of the belligerent powers has been virtually admitted by all.

The duty of holding a neutral conduct may be inferred, without anything more, from the obligation which justice and humanity impose on every nation, in cases in which it is free to act, to maintain inviolate the relations of peace and amity towards other nations.

The inducements of interest for observing that conduct will best be referred to your own reflections and experience. With me, a predominant motive has been to endeavor to gain time to our country to settle and mature its yet recent institutions, and to progress without interruption, to that degree of strength and consistency, which is necessary to give it, humanly speaking, the command of its own fortunes.

Though in reviewing the incidents of my administration, I am unconscious of intentional error—I am nevertheless too sensible of my